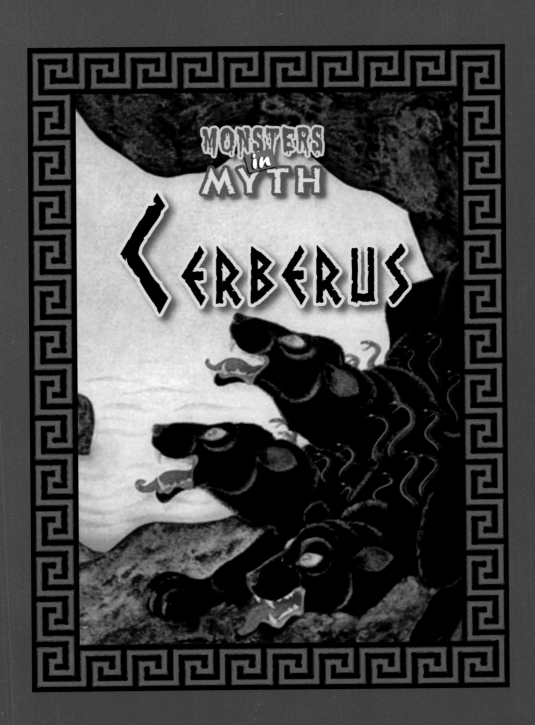

MONSTERS in MYTH

CERBERUS

MONSTERS in MYTH

TITLES IN THE SERIES

MONSTERS in MYTH

Cerberus

KATHLEEN TRACY

Mitchell Lane
PUBLISHERS

P.O. BOX 196
HOCKESSIN, DELAWARE 19707
VISIT US ON THE WEB: WWW.MITCHELLLANE.COM
COMMENTS? EMAIL US: MITCHELLLANE@MITCHELLLANE.COM

Mitchell Lane

PUBLISHERS

Printing   1   2   3   4   5   6   7   8   9

Library of Congress Cataloging-in-Publication Data
Tracy, Kathleen.
  Cerberus / by Kathleen Tracy.
      p. cm. — (Monsters in myth)
  Includes bibliographical references (p.   ) and index.
  ISBN 978-1-58415-924-7 (library bound)
  1. Cerberus (Greek mythology)—Juvenile literature. I. Title.
  BL820.C4T73 2011
  398.20938'01—dc22
                                                                2010026968

ABOUT THE AUTHOR: : Kathleen Tracy has been a journalist for over twenty years. Her writing has been featured in magazines including *The Toronto Star*'s "Star Week," *A&E Biography*, *KidScreen*, and *TV Times*. She is also the author of numerous books for Mitchell Lane Publishers, including *Odysseus* and *Theseus*. Tracy lives in the Los Angeles area with her two dogs and African Grey parrot.

AUTHOR'S NOTE: In this book, the Roman version of the hero's name, Hercules, has been used. It is the one by which most Americans know him. To the Greeks, he was known as Heracles (HAYR-uh-kleez). Other characters and places in this story are given their Greek names. Though based on the myths, dialogue and specific events in this book are imagined—just as the dialogue and events in myths are imagined.

PUBLISHER'S NOTE: This story is based on the author's extensive research, which she believes to be accurate. Documentation of such research is contained on page 46.
    The internet sites referenced herein were active as of the publication date. Due to the fleeting nature of some web sites, we cannot guarantee they will all be active when you are reading this book.
    To reflect current usage, we have chosen to use the secular era designations BCE ("before the common era") and CE ("of the common era") instead of the traditional designations BC ("before Christ") and AD (*anno Domini*, "in the year of the Lord").

TABLE OF CONTENTS

MONSTERS IN MYTH

CERBERUS

There have been many different depictions of Cerberus. In some, he is shown to have one head of a dog, one of a lion, and one of a wolf. In most, such as this nineteenth-century watercolor by William Blake, he is a three-headed hound.

CERBERUS

CHAPTER 1

Hound of Hell

The huge dog sprawled on the ground, its three heads resting on massive front paws. At first glance the animal was so still it appeared dead . . . until the thick tail twitched, revealing itself to be a snake. At the whispering of shifting sand, an eye on one of the great heads slid open. Although the creature remained motionless, it was alert and watchful.

When the sound grew louder the creature lifted his head, turning to peer into the murky mist leading to the world above, ears tense, listening. The movement roused the other heads, which gazed up and down the banks of the River Styx (STIKS). Through the haze a figure slowly emerged. A deep growl rumbled from the dog, shaking the ground. The creature rose gracefully from the ground, the three heads bobbing as if attached to the hound's enormous neck by springs. On its back, a swarm of snakes also awoke, turning into a mass of rasping scales.

When the figure became clear, with the full beard and dark hair falling down over his forehead, the dog relaxed and loped toward the man. It was Hades (HAY-deez), god of the Underworld and the dog's master.

Hades' expression was gloomy as he reached out to stroke the dog's heads. Cerberus (SUR-ber-us, or KER-ber-us) was Hades' faithful watch-dog. He kept souls from leaving the Underworld once they arrived and prevented humans from venturing in by eating them. Cerberus was almost as feared by mortals as Hades was.

Cerberus was happy to see his master, but he was also a little disappointed—he was hungry. Ravenous. He had hoped his visitor would be a mortal trying to sneak into the Underworld; Cerberus had developed a particular taste for live meat.

It wasn't Cerberus's job to think; it was his job to guard. Still, he sometimes wondered why anyone would want to sneak into the Underworld. It was not a happy place. Souls lived as shadows, unable to remember anything about the lives they had led aboveground. Most of them didn't suffer but existed in a state of nothingness—for eternity. The exceptions were the souls in the Elysian Fields, which were reserved for special mortals, such as heroes. In the Elysian Fields, souls lived happily. They remembered everything about their lives and were allowed to enjoy many of the pleasures from their mortal world, such as wine, music, and laughter. They were the lucky few.

With a weary sigh, Hades left, heading back to the palace he shared with his wife, Persephone (per-SEH-fuh-nee). Cerberus paced back and forth in front of the gates to the Underworld, lunging with his razor-sharp teeth bared at any soul that came too close to the entrance. When Charon (KAYR-on) the boatman brought another group of souls across the River Styx, Cerberus sat apart, tail wagging, and watched with one head as the recently deceased filed in to see the judges of the Underworld; the other two heads kept watch on the gate. As the boat drifted back into the mist, Cerberus started pacing again, stomach growling.

Cerberus had no concept of time, so it could have been a minute later or a decade later, but the beast stopped suddenly, all three heads sniffing the dank air. Mixed with the familiar mustiness of the sun-starved Underworld was a strange bouquet of new scents. The watchdog recognized the smell of a mortal and the lingering perfume of the world above. There was another strange odor that the dog instinctively knew was an animal, but he didn't know what kind.

Agitated, Cerberus began to pace more quickly, his serpent tail darting restlessly, the snakes on his back hissing loudly. Something wasn't right, and the three heads strained with tension, waiting for the confrontation Cerberus sensed was imminent. This was no soul approaching from inside the gates to the Underworld, nor was it Hades returning from above.

As Cerberus watched, a mortal wearing a lion's skin emerged from the gates. *How did he get in without passing me?* the dog wondered, irritated. Powerfully built, the man carried no weapon, but his eyes glinted with confidence, as if he were the predator and Cerberus the prey. Rage coursed through Cerberus, sending the snakes into a slithering frenzy.

Hades' watchdog did not know he was facing the great hero Hercules (HER-kyoo-leez), who needed to capture Cerberus in order to complete

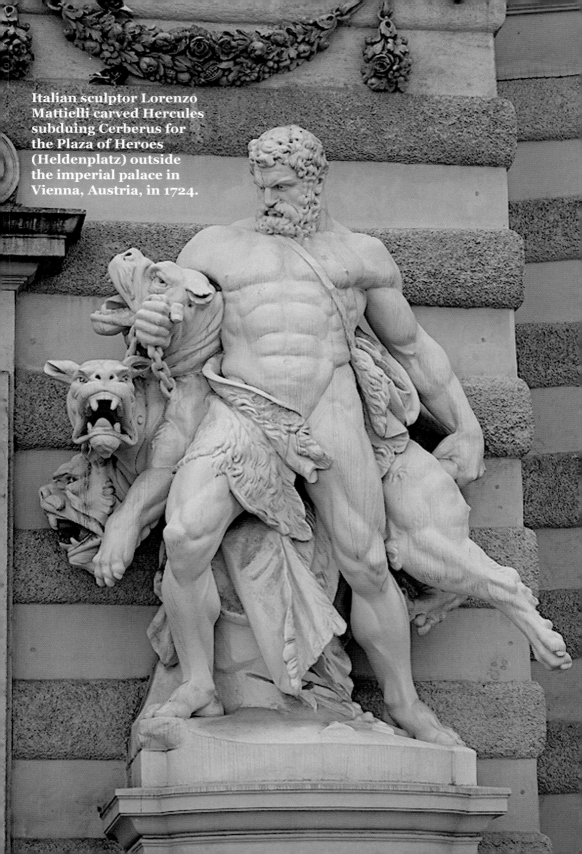

Italian sculptor Lorenzo Mattielli carved Hercules subduing Cerberus for the Plaza of Heroes (Heldenplatz) outside the imperial palace in Vienna, Austria, in 1724.

Hercules presents Eurystheus with the frightening hellhound on an Etruscan vase from around 530–525 BCE.

the last of his great labors—twelve superhuman feats to atone for having caused the death of his beloved family.

The creature snarled as Hercules slowly circled, and poisonous saliva dripped from the sides of its three fearsome mouths. When Hercules lunged at him, Cerberus swiped at the man, but his claws had no effect on the lion's skin. Furious, Cerberus clamped his jaws on the man's arm, and his snake-headed tail struck his side. The protective hide was impenetrable.

After an epic struggle, Cerberus felt the powerful hands of Hercules closing around his throats. Unable to breathe, he stopped struggling. He felt the cold weight of chains as Hercules wrapped them around his body. When the hero threw the animal over his shoulders to carry him out of the Underworld, the dog's furious howls echoed off the walls of hell.

Hades and Persephone

Persephone was the daughter of Demeter (DIH-mih-ter), goddess of the harvest, and Zeus (ZOOS), ruler of all the Greek gods. Demeter was devoted to her only child. Happy and well-behaved, Persephone was called Kore (KOR-ee) as a girl, which means "young maiden." By the time she was a teenager, Persephone had grown into a beautiful young woman.

One day when Hades was aboveground, he happened to see Persephone picking flowers beside a lake. According to mythology scholar Thomas Bulfinch, Hades "saw her, loved her, and carried her off. She screamed for help to her mother and companions."[1] He took her to Tartarus before anyone could help and made her queen of the Underworld.

Demeter had heard Persephone's terrified screams but her daughter was already gone by the time she arrived at the lake. Fearful of Hades, nobody told Demeter what had happened. Panic-stricken, she searched the earth in vain trying to find her daughter. Eventually Demeter grew despondent—and angry. She blamed the land for apparently swallowing up her child. "Ungrateful soil, which I have endowed with fertility and clothed with herbage and nourishing grain, no more shall you enjoy my favors."[2]

Demeter turned the land barren, and no crops or plants grew. Without grass, the cattle died, too, and people were starving. Eventually, she learned the truth and went to confront Zeus, demanding he get Persephone back. Zeus agreed but only if Persephone had not eaten anything, for anyone who ate in the Underworld was forbidden to leave.

Some myths say that in the time Persephone had been in the Underworld, she had grown to care for Hades. She missed her mother terribly and her life on earth but also liked being queen. Although she had eaten a few pomegranate seeds, a compromise was worked out so that famine would not kill mankind. Persephone was allowed to spend half the year with her mother, then she would spend the other half with Hades. Demeter agreed, and during the time her daughter was with her, the earth was bountiful. When Persephone returned to Hades, the earth became barren again. The Greeks told this story as a way of explaining the seasons.

Hades capturing Persephone

The Battle Between the Gods and the Titans, 1600, by Joachim Wtewael. The Greeks believed the first gods on earth were the Titans, who were created when the world was formed. The Titans were overthrown by their children, known as the Olympian gods and led by Zeus.

CERBERUS

CHAPTER 2

Creation

Like many of the monsters in Greek mythology, Cerberus could trace his lineage back to the creation of the world. One of the best-known accounts of the ancient Greeks' view of creation is Hesiod's *Theogony*.

The universe began with Chaos. Hesiod describes him as the first being but doesn't say much else. When Greece became a Roman province in 149 BCE, the Romans adopted Greek mythology as their own. The deities they had believed in took on Greek characteristics, but in many cases the Romans kept the names of their own gods. The Roman poet Ovid, who was born in 43 BCE, is more descriptive of Chaos than Hesiod. Ovid writes:

> Before there was earth or sea or the sky that covers every-thing, Nature appeared the same throughout the whole world: what we call chaos: a raw confused mass, nothing but inert matter, badly combined discordant atoms of things, confused in the one place. . . . Though there was land and sea and air, it was unstable land, unswimmable water, air needing light. Nothing retained its shape, one thing obstructed another, because in the one body, cold fought with heat, moist with dry, soft with hard, and weight with weightless things.[1]

He goes on to describe the formation of the earth, sky, and sea by an unnamed god who separated the world into five zones.

> When he had disentangled the elements, and freed them from the obscure mass, he fixed them in separate spaces in harmonious peace. . . . Just as the heavens are divided into

two zones to the north and two to the south, with a fifth and hotter between them, so the god carefully marked out the enclosed matter with the same number, and described as many regions on the earth. The equatorial zone is too hot to be habitable; the two poles are covered by deep snow; and he placed two regions between and gave them a temperate climate mixing heat and cold.[2]

From Chaos (Confusion) came Gaia (Earth), Tartarus (the Underworld), and Eros (Love). Hesiod refers to these four as the deathless gods.

From Gaia, through parthenogenesis, came Ourea (OOR-ee-uh), the mountains; Pontus (PON-tus), the sea; and Uranus (YUR-uh-nus), the upper sky, or heaven. Uranus was Gaia's equal and together produced many offspring, including the Titans, who became known as the Elder gods. The Titans were eventually overthrown by the Olympian gods, led by Zeus. The Titans were then imprisoned in Tartarus, the abyss of the Underworld.

Generally speaking, Tartarus sired monsters, but there are two main genealogies about the lineage of the best-known monsters. According to Hesiod, with Pontus, Gaia spawned Ceto (KEE-toh) and Phorcys (FOR-kis), who were the gods of large sea creatures.

Phorcys married his sister Ceto and they had several monster children such as Ladon, a hundred-headed serpent; the sea foam spirits, the Graeae (GRAY-eye); the Gorgons, including Medusa; and the dragon Echidna (eh-KID-nuh).

According to Greek mythographer Apollodorus, Echidna was the offspring of Gaia and Tartarus. Whoever her parents, Echidna was a *drakaina*—half woman and half serpent. In some accounts she is half dragon. She presided over rot, slime, dirty water, and disease. She resided in the swampy, dank regions of the Underworld and was so fearful a creature that the gods morphed into animals at the sight of her and fled in fear.

Although in at least one account, Echidna's mate, Typhon, was the son of Hera alone, others concur that he was the child of Gaia and Tartarus. He was a storm giant—so big that his head brushed the stars. From the

A Roman mosaic shows Phorcys and Ceto, the grandparents of Cerberus. Phorcys was sometimes called the Old Man of the Sea. He and his sister Ceto bore many monsters, who in turn bore another generation of monsters. These broods would challenge heroes throughout the mythology of Greece and Rome.

thighs up he was human in form; from the thighs down were two vipers for legs. Instead of fingers, he had fifty snakes attached to each hand. Fire would spew from his mouth when he opened it. He is sometimes depicted as winged with pointed ears, a dirty beard, and matted hair. Typhon and Echidna parented frightful creatures, including the Chimaera, the Sphinx, the Hydra, the two-headed canine Orthus (or Orthrus), and Cerberus.

Typhon was Gaia's youngest offspring, born after her first children, the Titans, had been made prisoners in the Underworld. Upset at how Zeus treated the Titans, Gaia convinced Typhon to challenge Zeus. A terrible battle followed, killing almost every living creature on earth. Typhon ripped Mount Etna out of the ground, but before he could hurl it, Zeus

Typhon was a fire-breathing monster who was so tall, his head could touch the stars. With his arms outstretched, one hand touched East and the other, West.

Mount Etna, located on the island of Sicily, is the largest active volcano in Europe. The ancient Greeks believed that Zeus imprisoned Typhon beneath the mountain. Still angry, Typhon occasionally spits fire in the form of volcanic eruptions.

struck it with his thunderbolts. The mountain fell back to earth, trapping Typhon beneath it, turning Mount Etna into a volcano.

Echidna escaped destruction. She hid in a cave and protected her children. Rather than destroy them, Zeus let the monsters live so that they could be used as challenges to future heroes. Nobody would confront, and defeat, as many monsters as Hercules, which is why many Greeks considered him the greatest hero of all.

F.Y.I.
FOR YOUR INFORMATION

Monstrous Family

Echidna was the mother of some of the most famous, and infamous, monsters in Greek mythology. However fearsome they were, most eventually met their demise at the hands of a hero.

The Caucasian (kaw-KAY-zhun) eagle was one of Echidna's offspring. After the Titan Prometheus gave the gift of fire to humans, an irate Zeus punished him by tying him to a boulder in the Caucasus Mountains. Every day the Caucasian eagle ripped him open to feed on his liver. At night his liver would grow back, only to be eaten by the eagle again come morning. Eventually Hercules killed the eagle and freed Prometheus.

Atlas watches the Caucasian eagle eat Prometheus' liver.

The fierce Nemean lion had impenetrable skin. Hercules strangled the beast. Using the monster's claws, he skinned it and used the hide as armor and the head as a helmet.

A horrible two-headed dog, Orthus (or Orthrus) belonged to the Titan Geryon, who had three bodies attached at the waist. Orthus and a shepherd named Eurytion (yoo-RIH-tee-on) guarded Geryon's precious red cattle. To complete one of his labors, Hercules killed Orthus, Eurytion, and Geryon and stole the cattle.

The death of Orthus

Hercules wearing the Nemean lion's hide

The Hydra was a snake with many heads, one of them immortal. The other heads could be cut off, but when that

F.Y.I.
FOR YOUR INFORMATION

Slaying the Hydra

happened two more grew in its place. Hercules killed the monster by cutting off the mortal heads and cauterizing the wounds so that new heads could not grow back. Then he cut off the immortal head and buried it. He cut open the corpse and dipped his arrows into the poisonous blood to use on future foes.

The Crommyonian (kroh-mee-OH-nee-un) sow was a giant wild pig named Phaea (FAY-uh) that preyed on the residents of Attica. In one of his early adventures, Theseus killed her.

The fire-breathing Chimaera (ky-MAYR-uh) had three parts, with a head for each part. The front of her body was a lion, her midsection was a goat, and her tail was a snake. She would meet her match in the hero Bellerophon.

The Sphinx had the body of a lion, the torso and head of a woman, and the wings of an eagle. In some depictions, she also had a serpent's tail. She terrorized the city of Thebes, devouring citizens who could not answer her riddle. When Oedipus (EH-dih-pus) answered it correctly, she hurled herself from her perch to her death.

The Chimaera

The Sphinx

21

Eleusis is near the Temple of Demeter, the mother of Persephone. The ancient Greeks believed the area held one of the entrances to the Underworld and was the route Hades took when he kidnapped Persephone.

CERBERUS

CHAPTER 3

The Underworld

The ancient Greeks believed that after a person died, their spirit—called a shade by the Greeks—went to the Underworld. Hades, which was what the Greeks called the Underworld as well as the god who ruled it, was also called Erebus (AYR-uh-bus; Darkness). All who entered Hades had to stay there and, with few exceptions, no mortals were allowed in. It was Cerberus's job to make sure the dead stayed in and the living stayed out.

In Homer's *Odyssey*, the Underworld is said to be located beyond the western horizon, and the Greeks believed it had several entrances. According to Greek geographer Strabo, there was "a headland that projects into the sea, Taenarum, with its temple of Poseidon situated in a grove; and secondly, near by, to the cavern through which, according to myth writers, Cerberus was brought up from Hades by Heracles."[1] Other entrances were through the Alcyonian Lake at Lerna and Lake Avernus near Naples.

There were five rivers encircling Hades: Styx, Acheron, Phlegethon, Cocytus, and Lethe. The River Styx, the river of hate, formed the boundary between earth and the Underworld. Styx circled Hades nine times and eventually converged with the other rivers at the center of Hades in a huge swamp. According to some versions, Styx had miraculous powers and could make a human immortal. It is believed that the great warrior Achilles (uh-KIL-eez) was dipped into the river as a baby, making him invincible against any weapon. He was protected everywhere except for his heel, where his mother had held him while he was submerged.

The River Acheron is the river of pain and a branch of the River Styx. Recently departed souls had to be ferried across this river to enter Hades. In Epeirus, an underground River Acheron was thought to lead to the Underworld.

The River Phlegethon (Blazing) flowed with fire; it emptied into the River Acheron. The River Cocytus (koh-KY-tus), "wailing," was another branch of the Acheron.

In Greek, *lethe* means "forgetfulness." Some ancient Greeks believed that souls were made to drink from the River Lethe so that they would not remember their lives and pine for former loved ones.

The Greeks believed that when people died, the messenger god Hermes (HER-meez) guided their souls to the Underworld. Once there, he delivered them to Charon, the ferryman. Charon is typically depicted as a somber old man, similar to contemporary images of the Grim Reaper.

Charon was the son of Erebus and Nyx (NIKS)—Darkness and Night. Nyx was sometimes depicted with black or shadowy wings and was called "swift Night." She lived in the Underworld during the day and only came out at dusk. In *The Iliad*, Homer says she is the only goddess that Zeus dared not offend.[2] Other offspring of Erebus and Nyx were Aether (EYE-thur), Brightness; Hemera (hay-MAYR-uh), Day; Hypnos (HIP-nohs), Sleep; and Thanatos (THAN-uh-tohs), Death.

To get into the Underworld, the souls had to be ferried across the River Acheron (AK-uh-ron) by Charon—though in some later

Many artists, including Gustave Doré in the 1860s, depicted Charon as an old man.

myths, most notably Virgil's *Aeneid*, Charon ferries them across the River Styx. Virgil describes Charon as

> old and squalid, but strong and vigorous . . . receiving passengers of all kinds into his boat; magnanimous heroes, boys and unmarried girls as numerous as the leaves that fall at autumn or the flocks that fly southward at the approach of winter. They stood pressing for a passage and longing to touch the opposite shore. But the stern ferryman took in only such as he chose, driving the rest back. Aeneas, wondering at the sight, asked the Sibyl, "Why this discrimination?" She answered, "Those who are taken on board the bark are the souls of those who have received due burial rites; the host of others who have remained unburied are not permitted to pass the flood, but wander a hundred years, and flit to and fro about the shore, till at last they are taken over."[3]

Besides accepting only souls of the dead who had been properly buried, Charon also ferried only those with the money to pay him a fee. Souls that did not have the money were doomed to wander the banks of the Cocytus. Some accounts say they wandered for a hundred years, others say for eternity. The ancient Greeks and Romans buried their dead with a coin to ensure safe passage.

Once they crossed the river and entered the Underworld, they faced three judges—Aeacus (EE-uh-kus), Rhadamanthys (rad-uh-MAN-thus), and Minos (MY-nohs), who had all been great and fair kings while they lived. Depending on the person's actions while alive, the judges sent the soul to either Tartarus, the Plain of Asphodel, or, for a very chosen few, Elysium.

The worst place in Hades was the bronze-walled Tartarus, a deep, grim pit where it was believed all the world's rivers originated. The Greeks believed that it would take an anvil dropped from the heavens nine days to reach earth; an anvil dropped from earth would reach Tartarus on the tenth day.

At the entrance of Tartarus were huge bronze pillars that not even the gods could destroy. The worst sinners and criminals were sent there to be

THE ENTRANCES TO HADES

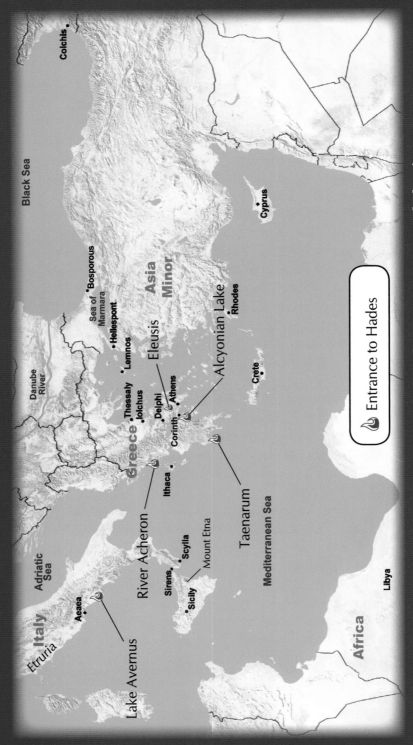

Colchis

Black Sea

Cyprus

Sea of 'Bosporous
Marmara
'Hellespont.

Asia Minor

Eleusis

Alcyonian Lake

Rhodes

Danube River

Lemnos

Thessaly
Jolchus

Delphi •Athens
Corinth

Greece

Crete

Ithaca .

Taenarum

Mediterranean Sea

River Acheron

Adriatic Sea

Sirens. Scylla
Mount Etna
Sicily.

Italy
Etruria

Aeaea

Lake Avernus

Libya

Africa

[Entrance to Hades] Entrance to Hades

The ancient Greeks believed that several caves, including those at Taenarum and Eleusis, were entrances to Hades. Several rivers of Hades had counterparts on the surface, including the River Styx in Lebadeia (between Delphi and Athens) and the River Acheron in Epeirus. These rivers disappeared underground, spawning the idea that they were portals to the Underworld.

In his 1588 painting *Fall of the Titans*, Cornelis van Haarlem shows the fate of the Titans—trapped in Tartarus for eternity.

punished for eternity. It was also where gods imprisoned monsters and their enemies. Zeus sent the Titans to Tartarus after defeating them to become ruler of the gods.

The vast majority of souls were sent to the Plain of Asphodel, a dark, damp, and cold area where the souls were neither tormented nor joyous; they just existed in a state of nothingness surrounded by faded images of their life on earth.

While the ancient Greeks did not fear the afterlife, it wasn't something to look forward to, either. The hero Achilles said, "I'd rather be a day-laborer on earth working for a man of little property than lord of all the hosts of the dead."[4]

In *The Odyssey*, Homer called the dead "pathetic in their helplessness, inhabiting drafty, echoing halls, deprived of their wits, and flitting purposelessly about uttering batlike noises."[5]

For a very few souls, though, the afterlife was one of bliss because they were allowed to go to Elysium, also called the Elysian Fields. According to Homer, Elysium was a paradise, located at the western end of the world, and filled with sunshine, gentle breezes, and happiness.

Famous Residents of Tartarus

The most famous residents of Tartarus fell into two general categories: sinner or enemy of a god. What they had in common were gruesome, eternal punishments.

Sisyphus (SIH-sih-fus), the founder and first king of Corinth, was known for his cleverness—and deviousness. He tied up Thanatos (Death) so that no one on earth could die. Another god, Ares, freed Thanatos, then sent Sisyphus to meet his own death. Before he died, Sisyphus instructed his wife, Merope (MER-oh-pee), not to give him a proper burial; that way he would not be admitted to the Underworld. Angry at the ploy, Hades sent him back to earth to ask her to perform proper burial rites. Sisyphus agreed to ask her, but instead stayed on earth until the end of his natural life. When he finally returned to the land of the dead, he was sentenced for eternity to push a large boulder uphill, only for the rock to roll back down when he neared the top.

Sisyphus, Franz von Stuck, 1920

Ixion (IK-see-on) murdered his father-in-law, and then tried to seduce Hera, the wife of Zeus. Zeus ordered Hermes to tie Ixion to a fiery wheel that never stopped spinning.

Tantalus (TAN-tuh-lus) was the son of Zeus and king of Sipylus. One version of his story says he angered Zeus by sharing ambrosia, the food of the gods, with mortals. The better-known story says the gods were upset after Tantalus invited them for dinner and, to test whether they really "know all," served the body of his son as the main course. His punishment was eternal hunger and thirst. Although immersed in water up to his neck, when he bent to drink, the water receded; fruit hung overhead, but when he stretched toward a piece of it, the wind blew the branches out of his reach. The word *tantalize* comes from Tantalus's punishment.

Ixion in Tartarus on the Wheel,
Bernard Picart, 1733

Tityus (TIH-tee-us) the giant was another son of Zeus. On Hera's orders, Tityus attempted to kill Leto, the mother of Zeus's children Artemis and Apollo. His punishment was much like that of Prometheus: Vultures and snakes eternally ripped him open to feed on his liver, which continuously regrew.

Hercules meets Cerberus in the Underworld. The son of
Zeus and Alcmene, Hercules was hounded by Zeus's
wife, Hera, for most of his life.

CERBERUS

CHAPTER 4

"Glorious Gift of Hera"

It was not easy being the wife of Zeus. The king of the gods was constantly sneaking around behind her back, being unfaithful with one beautiful woman after another. Hera's typical response was to get mad *and* to get even. Since there wasn't much she could do to Zeus, she took her revenge on the women or the children born from his affairs.

Alcmene (alk-MEE-nee) was an innocent victim of Zeus's deception. She was the daughter of King Electryon (ee-LEK-tree-on), who ruled over Mycenae. Her husband was Amphitryon (am-FIH-tree-on). Zeus became smitten with Alcmene, so he disguised himself as Amphitryon and seduced her while the real Amphitryon was away. Alcmene's husband discovered Zeus's ruse from an oracle, or psychic. In the end, Alcmene ended up carrying two children—one by Zeus and one by her husband.

She gave birth to two sons: Iphikles (IF-ih-kleez) and Heracles (HAYR-uh-kleez). (The Romans called him Hercules, which has become the more widely used form of the name.) Nobody knew which child was Amphitryon's and which was Zeus's, but they would soon figure it out.

Hera, still angry about Zeus's cheating, turned her anger on Alcmene's children. When the babies were about eight months old, she sent two huge snakes to kill them. Iphikles saw the serpents and began wailing in fear; Hercules grabbed the snakes by the neck and choked them until they died. It was clear by his superhuman strength that Hercules was the son of a god.

Alcmene and Amphitryon originally planned to name Zeus's son Alcaeus (al-KY-us), but after he killed the snakes, Alcmene called him Heracles, which means "Glorious Gift of Hera" in Greek. He would achieve greatness by overcoming struggles put in his path by Zeus's vengeful wife.

Even as an infant, Hercules displayed superhuman strength. When Hera sent snakes to kill Hercules and his twin brother Iphikles, Hercules killed the vipers, proving he was the son of a god.

Growing up, Hercules was not perfect, and he was known to have a bad temper. One day his tutor Linus reprimanded him for making mistakes during his music instruction and not paying close enough attention. Feeling the criticism was unjust, Hercules became enraged. He hit Linus with his lyre and killed him.

The display of violence alarmed Amphitryon. He sent Hercules away from their house to watch over the family flock of sheep in the countryside. Hercules spent the rest of his youth away from his family, growing into a tall, extremely powerful young man.

The Olympian gods were featured on the Parthenon, a temple dedicated to Athena in Athens. In the center are Zeus and Athena, and behind her is Hephaestus. Replicas of the Parthenon and its Olympic frieze have been made around the world.

When Hercules reached manhood at age eighteen, many of the Olympian gods gave him gifts. Zeus gave him an unbreakable shield, made by Hephaestus (heh-FES-tus), the god of the forge. Hephaestus also presented Hercules with a golden breastplate and protective footwear. Athena (uh-THEE-nuh), goddess of wisdom and war, gave him a helmet and a coat of arms. Apollo, the god of light, gave him a bow; Hermes gave him a sword; and the sea god Poseidon (poh-SY-dun) gave him a team of horses. No longer a boy, Hercules left the countryside.

When he got back home, Kreon, the king of Thebes, offered Hercules his daughter Megara's hand in marriage. Kreon also offered Iphikles the hand of Megara's sister.

There are more versions of Hercules' life and times than of any other character from Greek and Roman mythology. Some state he had three children with Megara; other versions say two children; and at least one

Delphi, considered the holiest temple in ancient Greece, was the home to an oracle, or seer, called the Pythia. The temple dates back to at least 1200 BCE.

says he had six children. What they can agree on is that Hercules was happy with Megara, but Hera refused to leave him alone and devised a new plan to ruin his life. She cast a spell that caused Hercules to become violently insane. While out of his mind, he killed his children. Some stories say Hercules also killed some of Iphikles' children. In many accounts, he also murdered Megara, while in others she was spared.

When he regained his senses, Hercules was despondent over killing his children. Because he was so admired by the people of Thebes, he was not punished for his crimes, but guilt drove him to leave the city to seek absolution. He went to Delphi to find out from Apollo what he needed to do. Through the god's oracle, or seer, Hercules learned he needed to complete ten labors (which later became twelve) in order to be absolved for the slaying of his family. After completing his labors, he would also become immortal.

Hercules was instructed to go see his cousin Eurystheus, king of Mycenae and Tiryns. He was the grandson of the great hero Perseus, as was Hercules. The cousins grew up rivals, and Hercules knew that Eurystheus would give him the most difficult tasks possible. It would take Hercules the next twelve years to finish his labors, many of which were linked in a way with Cerberus:

1. Bring Eurystheus the hide of the Nemean lion. Hercules strangled this sibling of Cerberus with his own hands.
2. Kill the Hydra of Lerna. Another Cerberus sibling, Hercules defeated this monster with the help of his nephew, Iolaus. When Eurystheus found out Iolaus had helped, he chose not to count the slaying of the Hydra as a labor.
3. Bring back the Hind of Ceryneia. A hind is a deer, and this deer was red with feet of bronze and antlers of gold. It took Hercules one year to capture this valuable animal. Because the deer belonged to the goddess Artemis, he had to capture it alive then return it once Eurystheus had seen it.
4. Capture the Wild Boar of Erymanthus (ayr-ih-MAN-thus). When Hercules brought the man-eating beast to Eurystheus, the king was so frightened he hid in a large pottery jar.

An Etruscan urn shows Eurystheus hiding from the boar in his pottery jar.

5. Clean the Augean Stables. Before starting this labor, King Augeas of Elis agreed to give Hercules 10 percent of his cattle herd if he completed the job successfully. Hercules diverted two nearby rivers so that the water flowed through the stables, cleaning them out. When Hercules returned to Mycenae, Eurystheus said this labor didn't count, either, because Hercules was paid for it.

6. Get rid of the Stymphalian birds. These flesh-eating birds had wings, beaks, and claws of bronze. Hercules scattered them by shaking a bronze rattle that Athena helped him make, then shot them out of the sky.

7. Capture the Cretan bull. When Hercules got to Crete, he wrestled the bull into submission and rode it back to Eurystheus. The king set the beast loose and it ended up in Marathon, where it terrorized the locals.

8. Capture the Horses of Diomedes (dy-AH-muh-deez). After subduing the man-eating mares, Hercules fed the horses their master.

9. Bring the Girdle of the Amazon Queen. It was easy to get his hands on the belt (girdle) of Queen Hippolyte (hih-PAH-lih-tee), leader of the Amazons, a tribe of female warriors. But when Hera started a vicious rumor about why he had come, the women took up arms, and Hercules ended up killing the queen. Eurystheus gave the belt to his daughter.

10. Fetch the Cattle of Geryon. Geryon was a Titan who had three bodies attached at the waist. To get the cattle, Hercules killed their herder Eurytion and strangled Orthus, Cerberus' sibling. He also killed Geryon with his poison arrows.

11. Bring back the Apples of the Hesperides. These golden apples belonged to Hera and were protected by Ladon, the uncle of Cerberus. It was while on this labor that Hercules freed Prometheus, who told the hero how to get the apples. He had to offer to hold up the world for Atlas while Atlas went to pluck three of the apples from the goddess' orchard.

Eurystheus was frustrated that Hercules had successfully completed every labor. Determined to see his cousin fail, he saved the most certainly impossible labor for last. If Hercules wanted to find redemption, he would literally have to go to hell and back.

The Oracle at Delphi

Located in a cave on Mount Parnassus, Delphi was home to an oracle called the Pythia and was considered the holiest temple of the ancient Greeks. As a religious shrine, the Oracle of Delphi dates back to at least 1200 BCE.

The first shrine at Delphi honored Gaia and was protected by a giant snake called Python. Apollo, the sun god, killed Python and took over the temple as a shrine for himself. The story symbolizes how Greek civilization evolved from primitive times.

Apollo was also the Greek god of prophecy, meaning he could foretell the future. He spoke through a priestess called the Pythia. Over the centuries, there were many Pythias, and they were all older women who had lived a pure life. There are many stories of heroes such as Hercules and Theseus consulting with the Oracle at Delphi, but she was also accessible to average citizens.

People traveled from all over Greece to find out what the future held. When Apollo's followers arrived at Delphi, they were required to register, then pay money as an offering. After hearing the question, the Pythia went down into the cave. According to Greek historian Plutarch, the priestess breathed in fumes rising from the floor of the cave, which put her into a trance. That's when she would communicate with Apollo.

The answers were never very direct; instead they were like a riddle, subject to different interpretations. If the person was completely confused, the Pythia would offer to provide another prophecy for an additional fee.

Sometimes, the priestess would be overcome by the vapors in the cave and return almost delirious. Modern historians assumed the fumes were myth, but around the year 2001, scientists discovered there really were gases, including ethylene, coming up into the cave from cracks in the cave floor.[1] When breathed, ethylene can produce a drug-like effect; the more a person breathes it, the greater the effect. Fortunately for the Pythia, once a person stops breathing ethylene, the effects quickly disappear.

The Pythia

Orpheus in the Underworld, by Jan Brueghel the Elder, painted in 1594, shows Orpheus meeting Hades and Persephone on their thrones. The musician was one of the few living people to travel to Hades.

CERBERUS

CHAPTER 5

The Eternal Cerberus

Although Cerberus was supposed to keep the living out of the Underworld, a few mortals, with the help of the gods, made the round trip.

Orpheus (OR-fee-us) was known as the greatest musician in all of Greece. His music was so charming, it could calm even the most vicious beast. After his wife died from a snake bite, Orpheus went to Hades to bring her back. He was able to get past Cerberus by playing the lyre and lulling the monster dog to sleep. Although Orpheus was allowed to return to the surface with his wife, he could not bear to wait to see his bride. As they ascended, he turned to see if she was behind him, and with despair watched her fade back into the Underworld.

In *The Aeneid*, the Roman poet Virgil recounts how Aeneas (uh-NEE-us) traveled to Hades with the Sibyl, a prophetess of Apollo, to visit his father. Once there, the Sibyl threw Cerberus a drugged piece of honey-cake (sop) that made him pass out.

> Grim Cerberus, who soon began to rear
> His crested snakes, and arm'd his bristling hair.
> The prudent Sibyl had before prepar'd
> A sop, in honey steep'd, to charm the guard;
> Which, mix'd with pow'rful drugs, she cast before
> His greedy grinning jaws, just op'd to roar.
> With three enormous mouths he gapes; and straight,
> With hunger press'd, devours the pleasing bait.
> Long draughts of sleep his monstrous limbs enslave;
> He reels, and, falling, fills the spacious cave.
> The keeper charm'd, the chief without delay
> Pass'd on, and took th' irremeable way.[1]

Psyche and Cerberus, by French illustrator Edmund Dulac. In Roman mythology, Psyche was so beautiful that even the goddess Aphrodite was jealous of her and tormented Psyche constantly. Aphrodite agreed to stop bothering Psyche if she would do one task: obtain a box of beauty from Persephone. In order to get past Cerberus, Psyche fed him drugged honey cakes, proving even hellhounds love treats.

The Romans tell a similar story about tossing Cerberus food for passage. The beautiful mortal Psyche (SY-kee, whose name means "Soul") was married to the love god Cupid (Eros), which angered Venus (the Roman version of Aphrodite—af-roh-DY-tee—the goddess of love). Venus sent Psyche on several death-defying missions, until at last she sent her to the Underworld to retrieve a box of beauty from Proserpine (Persephone). Psyche entered through the cave at Taenarum. She was able to get past Cerberus by giving him bread (or honeycakes). She also brought coins with her to pay her passage back and forth across the Styx. Once she retrieved the box and began her return journey, however, she ignored divine advice and opened the box. She slept as if she were dead, until Cupid came to bring her back to the land of the living. Jupiter (Zeus) made her immortal, which allowed the other deities to bless her marriage to

Charon and Psyche, by John Roddam Spencer Stanhope, 1883. Psyche followed the same route to the Underworld as Hercules, descending through the cave at Taenarum. Once there she paid Charon to ferry her to the Underworld and back.

Antonio Canova was commissioned to carve *Psyche Revived by Cupid's Kiss* in 1787. Without the kiss of her immortal lover, Psyche would not have made it out of the Underworld.

Cupid. If Cupid had not retrieved his bride, she would not have returned to the light of day.

Hercules got by Cerberus on his way in to the Underworld with the help of Hermes, who snuck him in. Deciding that honesty was his only option, he sought out Hades and Persephone to ask if he could borrow their beast. The queen of the Underworld was known to assist mortals who came to Hades on a quest. She was sympathetic to Hercules' dilemma, and with her support, Hades permitted Hercules to take Cerberus with him back to Mycenae—but only if he could do it without weapons so that Cerberus would not be hurt.

Hercules found Cerberus prowling on the shore of the Acheron. He grabbed the dog by his thick throat. Cerberus tried to attack Hercules with his tail, but Hercules' lion skin protected him. Desperate, Cerberus fought wildly, but, using his brute strength, Hercules was able to subdue him.

In some versions of the story, Hercules slung the animal over his shoulder and carried him away. In another version, he bound Cerberus in unbreakable chains and dragged him out of Hades into the upper world. When the light of day hit the dog's eyes, he struggled some more, barking in pain, his mouth frothing. As drops of his saliva hit the ground, it turned

In some versions of the story, Hercules binds Cerberus in chains.

into a poisonous plant called aconite (now it is known as wolfsbane). This poison would appear in other myths: Medea would try to use it to poison Theseus, for example.

Finally Hercules made it back to the palace with the monstrous dog. When Eurystheus saw the living, and very angry, Cerberus, he was so terrified he once again hid in his pottery jar until Hercules took the animal back to the Underworld.

The labors complete, Hercules would go on other adventures, but his life remained a series of difficulties, much of it instigated by Hera. In the end, he was taken to Olympus and made immortal, fulfilling the Oracle at Delphi's prophecy.

Wolfsbane, or aconite, is used in medicine and as a deadly poison.

He later married Hebe, the goddess of eternal youth, and eventually enjoyed a truce with Hera.

While not a god, Cerberus has enjoyed his own kind of immortality. He has been featured in many works of art and literature, both classical and modern. His depiction has been fairly consistent from Roman times on: with a mane of snakes, a serpent's tail, and three heads—one of a lion, one of a dog, and the other of a wolf. (Only Hesiod deviates by claiming Cerberus had fifty heads.) The three heads represent the past, the present, and the future.

In Dante's epic poem *Divine Comedy*, Cerberus shows up in the third circle of hell, where he tears apart souls who have committed the deadly sin of gluttony.

> Cerberus, a monster fierce and strange, with three throats, barks dog-like over those that are immersed in it. His eyes are red, his beard greasy and black, his belly wide, and clawed his hands; he clutches the spirits, flays and piece-meal renders them. When Cerberus, the great Worm, perceived us, he opened his mouth and showed his tusks: no limb of him kept still. My guide, spreading his palms, took up earth; and, with full fists, cast it into his ravening gullets. As the dog, that barking craves, and grows quiet when he bites his food, for he strains and battles only to devour it: so did those squalid visages of Cerberus the Demon, who thunders on the spirits so, that they would fain be deaf.[2]

In the poem, Cerberus still has scars from when Hercules captured him.

In 1687, astronomer Johannes Heveliusin named a constellation after Cerberus, which supposedly shows Hercules holding him.

In modern times, Cerberus is an especially popular character in video games such as Age of Mythology: The Titans and Final Fantasy VIII. He has also appeared in TV shows and films such as *Clash of the Titans*. In *Harry Potter and the Sorcerer's Stone*, the character of Fluffy is modeled after Cerberus. And in *Percy Jackson and the Olympians: The Lightning Thief*,

In *Dante's Inferno*, Cerberus guards the entrance of the third circle of hell, which houses gluttons. In order to get past the beast, Virgil throws dirt into the beast's three mouths, temporarily satisfying the hound's hunger so that they can pass.

Cerberus is mollified when Annabeth, daughter of Athena, throws a red rubber ball for him to fetch.

In all these depictions, Cerberus represents a protector. Even though he is a dangerous and potentially deadly monster, he is not seen as evil. By and large, he has come to be seen as the ultimate guard dog. As a result, he is arguably the most appreciated of any monster in Greek mythology.

Hellhounds

Moddey Dhoo

Like dragons, hellhounds are creatures found in literature, folklore, and mythologies from cultures everywhere on earth. While Cerberus may be the original and best-known hellhound, he has plenty of company.

The descriptions of hellhounds tend to be similar: large black dogs with glowing red or perhaps yellow eyes; supernatural strength and/or speed; and a vicious disposition. Supernatural creatures, they mostly guard a hellmouth or entrance to a world of the dead, so cemeteries are favorite places for hellhounds to prowl. In some cultures, seeing a hellhound or hearing it howl foretells someone's imminent death.

Hellhounds are very common in Celtic mythology, including Moddey Dhoo of the Isle of Man and Gwyllgi of Wales. In Mexican and Central American folklore, the black cadejo is a huge dog that hunts young men who are out late at night on rural roads.

Hellhounds show up in modern literature too: In Harry Potter there is a hellhound referred to as The Grim.

Chapter 1. Hound of Hell

1. Thomas Bulfinch, "Proserpine— Glaucus and Scylla,"*Bulfinch's Mythology*, Chapter VII, http://www.sacred-texts.com/cla/ bulf/bulf06.htm
2. Ibid.

Chapter 2. Creation

1. Ovid, *Metamorphoses*, translated by Anthony S. Kline, 2000. http://etext.virginia.edu/latin/ ovid/trans/Metamorph.htm
2. Ibid.

Chapter 3. The Underworld

1. Strabo, *The Geography of Strabo,* with an English translation by Horace Leonard Jones, Ph.D., LL.D. (London: William Heinemann, 1927), 8.5.1.
2. Homer, *The Iliad*, translated by Robert Fagles (New York: Viking Press, 1990), Book 14, lines 256– 61.
3. Thomas Bulfinch, "Proserpine— Glaucus and Scylla," *Bulfinch's Mythology*, http://www.sacred-texts.com/cla/ bulf/bulf06.htm

4. Homer, *The Odyssey*, translated by Samuel Butler (The Internet Classics Archive, 1994–2000), Book 11, lines 489–91. http://classics.mit.edu/Homer/ odyssey.11.xi.html
5. Ibid., Book 24, lines 5 ff. http://classics.mit.edu/Homer/ odyssey.24.xxiv.html

Chapter 4. "Glorious Gift of Hera"

1. John Roach, "Delphic Oracle's Lips May Have Been Loosened by Gas Vapors," *National Geographic*, August 14, 2001, http://news.nationalgeographic.com/ news/2001/08/0814_delphioracle. html

Chapter 5. The Eternal Cerberus

1. Virgil, *The Aeneid*, translated by John Dryden (New York: Penguin Books, 1997), http://classics.mit. edu/Virgil/aeneid.html
2. Dante Alighieri, *The Divine Comedy of Dante Alighieri*, translated by John D. Sinclair (New York: Oxford University Press, 1924), Inferno, Canto VI.

For Young Adults

McCaughrean, Geraldine. *Hercules*. Peterborough, NH: Cricket Books, 2005.

Redmond, Shirley Raye. *Cerberus*. Farmington Hills, MI: KidHaven, 2008.

Whiting, Jim. *Hercules*. Hockessin, DE: Mitchell Lane Publishers, 2008.

Works Consulted

Apollodorus. *The Library*. Translated by Sir James George Frazer. Loeb Classical Library, Volumes 121 & 122. Cambridge, MA: Harvard University Press; London: William Heinemann Ltd., 1921. http://www.theoi.com/Text/Apollodorus1.html#2

Bulfinch, Thomas. *Bulfinch's Mythology: The Age of Fable, or Stories of Gods and Heroes*. 1855. http://www.sacred-texts.com/cla/bulf/bulf06.htm

Dante Alighieri. *The Divine Comedy of Dante Alighieri*. Translated by John D. Sinclair. New York: Oxford University Press, 1924.

Hesiod. *The Shield of Heracles*. Translated Hugh G. by Evelyn-White. 1914. http://ancienthistory.about.com/library/bl/bl_text_hesiod_shield.htm

———. *The Theogony of Hesiod*. Translated by Hugh G. Evelyn-White. 1914. http://www.sacred-texts.com/cla/hesiod/theogony.htm

Homer. *The Iliad*. Translated by Robert Fagles. New York: Viking Press, 1990.

———. *The Odyssey*. Translated by Samuel Butler. The Internet Classics Archive, 1994–2000. http://classics.mit.edu/Homer/odyssey.html

Ovid. *Metamorphoses*. Translated by Anthony S. Kline. 2000. http://etext.virginia.edu/latin/ovid/trans/Metamorph.htm

Roach, John. "Delphic Oracle's Lips May Have Been Loosened by Gas Vapors." *National Geographic*, August 14, 2001. http://news.nationalgeographic.com/news/2001/08/0814_delphioracle.html

Strabo. *The Geography of Strabo*. With an English translation by Horace Leonard Jones, Ph.D., LL.D. (The Loeb Classical Library.) London: William Heinemann, 1928.

Virgil. *The Aeneid*. Translated by John Dryden. New York: Penguin Books, 1997. http://classics.mit.edu/Virgil/aeneid.html

On the Internet

Cerberus: Three-Headed Guard Dog of Hades
    http://www.theoi.com/Ther/KuonKerberos.html

The Life and Times of Hercules
    http://www.perseus.tufts.edu/Herakles/bio.html

Mystery Mag: "Moddey Dhoo of Peel Castle"
    http://www.mysterymag.com/earthmysteries/
    ?artID=411&page=article&subID=74

absolution (ab-suh-LOO-shun)—Official forgiveness for a crime, such as by a priest.

bark—A type of sailing vessel with three or more masts.

cauterize (KAW-ter-yz)—To seal a wound by burning the flesh.

fain—Be happy about; be desirous of.

gluttony (GLUH-tuh-nee)—The act of overeating to extreme levels.

immortality (im-or-TAL-ih-tee)—The ability to live forever.

irremeable (eer-ih-MEE-uh-bul)—Having no possibility of return.

lyre (LYR, or LEER)—A harp-like stringed instrument.

mollify (MAH-lih-fy)—To sooth the temper.

morph (MORF)—To change form.

mortal (MOR-tul)—A being that can die.

parthenogenesis (par-then-oh-JEN-ih-sis)—Reproduction without a partner.

Sibyl (SIH-bul)—A woman who tells the future; especially one who acts on behalf of Apollo.

squalid (SKAH-lid)—Filthy as a result of neglect.

visage (VIS-ij)—Face.